The All Occasion Card Book

Ornare®

Diny van de Lustgraaf

FORTE PUBLISHERS

Contents

Seventh printing December 2004
ISBN 90 5877 209 8

This is a publication from
Forte Publishers BV
P.O. Box 1394
3500 BJ Utrecht
The Netherlands

For more information about the creative
books available from Forte Uitgevers:
www.forteuitgevers.nl
Publisher: Marianne Perlot
Editor: Hanny Vlaar
Photography and digital image editing:
Fotografie Gerhard Witteveen, Apeldoorn,
the Netherlands
Cover and inner design:
Studio Herman Bade BV, Baarn,
the Netherlands

Preface

This was a wonderful book to make. The only thing I found difficult was making sure I could fit

all the patterns into the book. The book has a limited number of pages and, of course, the

instructions had to be included as well. But thanks to Hanny, our editor-in-chief, we managed it.

Ornare The All Occasion Card Book is the result and it is full of cards for every occasion. This

book contains the pattern of every card. Some patterns have been used more than once and

I know that whilst making the cards, you will have new ideas of how you can use these patterns.

And in these busy times, where people rush from one thing to the next, making these cards will

help you to relax. Have fun!

I hope you enjoy making the cards.

Techniques

pattern 2

Copy the pattern and then stick this on the card using non-permanent adhesive tape. Pierce the pattern, making sure to keep the piercer vertical, otherwise the holes will not look very nice. Also make sure you push the piercer all the way through so that the holes are all the same size. You can cut the pattern out along the line. Next, remove the pattern. The back of the card, where the piercer comes out, is the good side of the pattern. The patterns can be used more than once. Always remember you are working on the back of the card and the pattern you see is, therefore, a mirror image. If, for example, you wish to have a corner pattern in the bottom left-hand corner, then you must pierce this in the bottom right-hand corner of the back of the card. Sometimes, you have to pierce a line of holes. There is no pattern for this, because this is very easy to do yourself. Whilst piercing, place a ruler on the card and use this to help you keep the line of holes nice and straight.

Most of the pictures used are stuck on the card using two layers. This will not be stated with the instructions given with the cards. The cutting patterns are not shown, because it is obvious how the pictures are stuck on the card. Cut out the whole picture for the first layer, and for the second layer, only cut out what is in the foreground. Stick the cut out pictures on top of each other using small pieces of 3D foam tape.

All the pictures are decorated with a thin layer of glitter. This will not be stated with the instructions given with the cards.

The size of the patterns has meant that they cannot be shown in the correct order. Just go a few pages forwards or backwards and you will find the pattern.

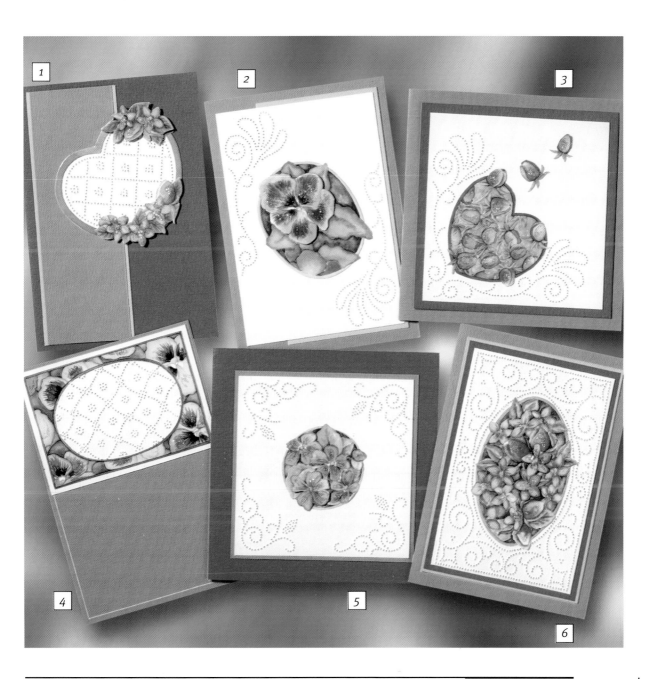

Materials

- ❏ *Papicolor card (the colours and colour numbers are given at the start of each chapter)*
- ❏ *Ornare cutting sheets*
- ❏ *Ornare piercer and piercing mat*
- ❏ *Ruler*
- ❏ *Pencil*
- ❏ *3D scissors*
- ❏ *Photo glue*
- ❏ *Non-permanent adhesive tape*
- ❏ *3D foam tape*
- ❏ *Glitter glue: sparkles (GW212) and silver (GW211)*

❏ Ornare piercer and piercing mat
The piercer has a thin, sharp point and the piercing mat is thick and strong enough to allow you to push the piercer into it.

❏ Card
Papicolor card is mostly used, but green card by Canson Mi-Teintes is used a couple of times. A parchment coloured card is also used a couple of times.

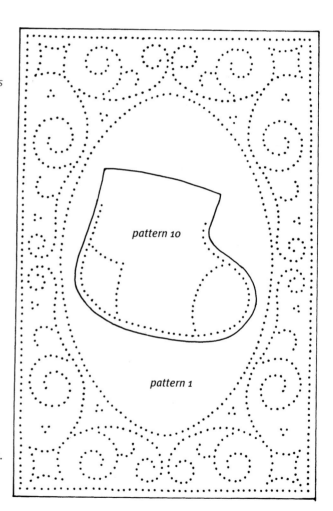

pattern 10

pattern 1

pattern 5

Flowers

carnation white card (9 x 13 cm). Use the top corner of the pattern as the corner of the card (not the bottom corner). Stick the picture in the middle of the card at an angle and stick this on caramel card (7 x 13.5 cm) and then on a violet double card.

What you need:
- ❏ *carnation white (no. 03), caramel (no. 26), cerise (no. 33) and violet (no. 20) (Papicolor)*
- ❏ *Ornare cutting sheets (OK032 and OK033)*
- ❏ *Sparkles glitter glue*
- ❏ *White fine-liner*

1. Heart on a portrait card

Pierce pattern 5 in carnation white card. Cut it out so that it is a couple of millimetres bigger than the outline and stick the picture on it. Stick a strip of violet card (4.5 x 14.2 cm) on caramel card (5 x 14.2 cm) and stick this on a cerise double card. Stick the heart on the card.

2. Violet

Pierce pattern 3 (page 23) in the bottom left-hand corner and the top right-hand corner of

3. Heart on a square card

Pierce pattern 3 (page 23) twice (one a mirror image of the other) in carnation white card (10.5 x 10.5 cm). Use the bottom corner of the pattern as the corner of the card (not the top corner). Stick the cut out heart in this pattern and then stick this on cerise card (11.5 x 11.5 cm). Finally, stick this in the bottom left-hand corner of a caramel card (13 x 13 cm).

4. Violet border

Place the cut out violet border in the middle of carnation white card (7 x 10 cm). Use a pencil to copy the oval and pierce pattern 2 (page 4) in this. Use a white fine-liner to draw a line around a violet card and stick everything on the right-hand side of the card.

continued on page 48

Birth

pattern 8

What you need:
- ❏ *Card: carnation white (no. 03), marigold (no. 10), azure (no. 04), blossom (no. 34) and brick red (no. 35) (Papicolor)*
- ❏ *Ornare cutting sheets (OK004 and OK025)*
- ❏ *Sparkles glitter glue*

1. Socks

Pierce pattern 10 (page 6) in carnation white card and cut it out. Pierce pattern 11 (page 10) in blue card and cut this out as well. Stick the parts of the socks on each other. Stick the cut out picture on red card (9 x 9 cm) (slightly towards the top) and then on blue card (9.5 x 9.5 cm). Stick this on a yellow double card. Stick the socks on the front of the card.

2. It's a boy

Pierce pattern 6 (page 10) in carnation white card and cut it out. Stick this on yellow card and cut it out so that there is a small yellow border at the top and bottom. Stick this and the two cut out pictures on a blue double card.

3. Baby

Pierce pattern 8 in yellow card and cut it out. Stick this on the cut out picture. Stick this on red card (11 x 11 cm) and then on carnation white card (11.5 x 11.5 cm). Finally, stick this on a blossom double card.

4. Sleeping peacefully with a teddy bear

Only pierce the inner and outer borders of pattern 9 (page 10) in carnation white card. Cut the oval out of the middle and cut along the edges of the pierced holes. Stick this on yellow card (8.5 x 12 cm) and then on a red double card. Stick the picture in the middle.

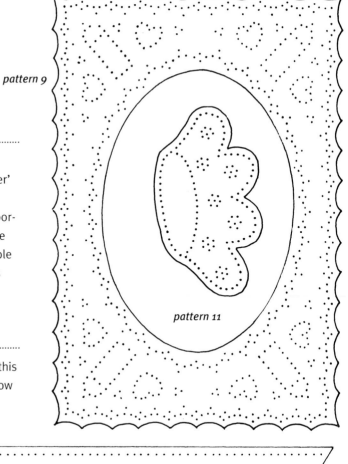

pattern 9

5. *It's a girl*

Pierce pattern 6 (page 10) in carnation white
card, but replace the word 'son' with 'daughter'
(pattern 7, page 11). Stick this on yellow card
and cut it out so that there is a small yellow border at the top and bottom. Stick a 3.5 cm wide
strip of brick red card at an angle on the double
card and cut off the excess. Stick the pictures
and the pattern on the card.

6. *On the scales*

Pierce pattern 9 in carnation white card. Stick this
on blue card (8.5 x 12.5 cm) and then on a yellow
double card. Stick the picture in the middle.

pattern 11

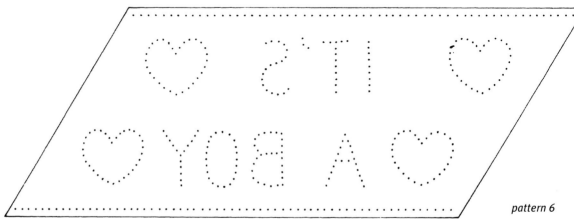

pattern 6

pattern 12

pattern 7

pattern 14

pattern 13

pattern 16

Party

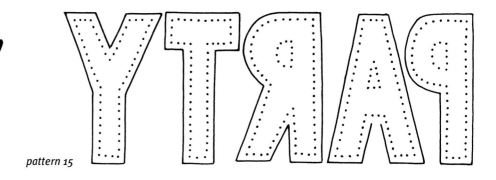

pattern 15

What you need:
- ❏ Card: carnation white (no. 03),
  marigold (no. 10), fiesta red (no. 12),
  dark blue (no. 06) and dark green (no. 16)
  (Papicolor)
- ❏ Ornare cutting sheets (OK008 and OK023)
- ❏ Silver glitter glue

1. Party in a square

Pierce the letters of pattern 15 in red card and cut them out. Stick the pictures in the corners of blue card (10.5 x 10.5 cm) and stick the letters in the middle.
Stick this on yellow card (11.5 x 11.5 cm) and then on a square green double card.

2. Champagne glasses

Pierce pattern 12 (page 11) twice in carnation white card and cut out the patterns. Stick green card (8 x 13 cm) on a yellow double card and stick the pictures and the patterns on it.

3. Good luck

Pierce pattern 14 (page 11) in the back of the cut out picture. Stick this on green card (8 x 8 cm) and then on a red double card.

4. Party

Pierce pattern 15 in blue card and cut out the letters. Pierce a border (along a ruler) around the edge of a green card (9 x 9 cm). Stick this on red card (10 x 10 cm) and then at the top of a yellow double card. Stick the pictures on the green card and stick the letters at the bottom of the yellow card.

5. Cakes

Cut a rectangle which is the same size as the outline of pattern 16 (page 11) out of the front of a red double card. Place a carnation white card (10 x 14.5 cm) under the opening and use a

continued on page 48

Christmas landscapes

pattern 18

What you need:

❏ *Card: snowy white (no. 30), night blue (no. 41)*
   (Papicolor) and parchment
❏ *Ornare cutting sheets (OK028 and OK029)*
❏ *Gold holographic origami paper*
❏ *Sparkles glitter glue*

1. Star with two strips

Cut two strips (2.5 x 9.5 cm) out of the front of
a blue double card (0.5 cm from the top and bottom edges of the card). Pierce a part of the long
side of pattern 16 (page 11) twice in white card
(2 x 9 cm). Stick these on origami paper (10.2 x
14.5 cm) which is stuck behind the openings in
the card. Stick the cut out picture on origami
paper. Cut it out with a border and stick this in
the middle of the card.

2. Star with curls

Pierce pattern 3 (page 23) in one of the short
sides of a white card (9.5 x 12.5 cm) and pierce
the pattern again in the bottom long side of the
card. Pierce a number of holes in a straight line
(along a ruler) in the opposite corner. Stick this
on dark blue card (10 x 13 cm) and then on a
parchment double card. Stick the cut out picture
on the origami paper. Cut it out with a border
and stick this on the card.

3. Shining star

Pierce pattern 21 in the middle of white card
(12 x 12 cm). Stick another copy of the pattern on
the front of a square blue double card and cut
along the lines. Stick the pierced pattern behind
the openings. Stick the cut out picture on origami paper. Cut it out with a border and stick this in
the middle of the card.

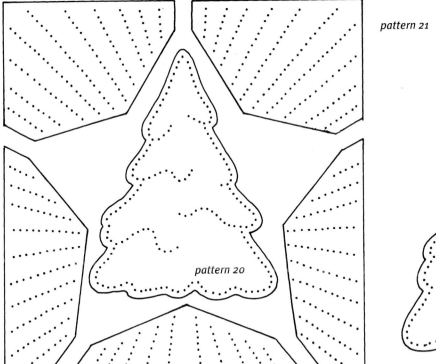

pattern 21 *pattern 19*

pattern 20

4. Looking through an arch

Pierce pattern 17 (page 19) in white card and cut it out. Stick this on blue card and cut it out so that there is a border.
Stick the cut out picture on origami paper and cut this out so that there is a border. Stick the picture on the pattern and then stick everything on a parchment double card.

5. Landscape with two stars

Pierce the stars of pattern 18 in white card and cut them out. Stick the stars and blue card (9.5 x 14 cm) on origami paper and cut them out so that there is a border. Stick the cut out picture and the stars on the blue card and stick this on a parchment double card.

6. Landscape with Christmas trees

Pierce the trees of patterns 19 and 20 in white card and cut them out.
Stick parchment (7.5 x 10 cm) on origami paper and cut this out so that there is a border. Stick the cut out picture on the parchment and stick this on a blue double card. Finally, stick the trees on the card.

Fun on the ice

pattern 22

What you need:

❏ *Card: snowy white (no. 30), night blue*
   (no. 41) and ice blue (Papicolor)
❏ *3D cutting sheets (3D384 and 3D385)*
❏ *Sparkles glitter glue*

1. Happy Christmas

Pierce pattern 17 in white card and cut it out. Stick this on night blue card and cut it out so that there is a border. Use a pencil to copy the opening on the front of an ice blue double card and cut this out so that it is a bit bigger. Stick the pattern on the card and stick the cut out picture in the opening.

2. Merry Christmas

Pierce pattern 22 in white card and cut it out. Stick the cut out picture on a strip of ice blue card (3 x 10 cm) and stick this on a night blue double card. Draw a line around the border using a white gel pen. Finally, stick the pattern on the card.

3. Taking a break

Pierce the bottom of pattern 23 (page 23) on the bottom of white card (8.5 x 13 cm) (ignore the line in the middle). Pierce the top of pattern 23 in the top of the card (also ignoring the line). Pierce a line of holes all around the card. Stick the cut out picture on the pattern and stick the pattern on night blue card (9 x 13.5 cm). Finally, stick this on an ice blue double card.

4. Making a snowman

Cut two rectangles (4.5 x 8.5 cm) out of night blue double card, 1 cm from the short sides. Place white card in the card and copy the openings using a pencil. Pierce the left-hand side

of pattern 23 (page 23) in the left-hand opening and pierce the right-hand side of the pattern in the right-hand opening (don't forget you are working on a mirror image). Stick this behind the front of the card. Draw lines around the opening using a white gel pen and stick the picture on the card.

5. Falling on the ice

Pierce pattern 23 (page 23) in white card and cut it out (ignore the line in the middle). Stick this on night blue card (9 x 9 cm) and then on ice blue card (11 x 11 cm). Stick all of this on a white double card. Stick the cut out picture on the card.

6. Sledding

Pierce the trees of patterns 19 and 20 (page 15) in white card and cut them out. Draw lines around the top and sides of night blue card (8 x 13.5 cm) using a white gel pen and stick this on an ice blue double card. Stick the two trees and the cut out picture on the card.

Marriage

pattern 27

What you need:

❏ *Card: carnation white (no. 03), violet (no. 20),*
  blossom (no. 34) and wine red (no. 36) (Papicolor)
❏ *Ornare cutting sheets (OK022 and OK007)*
❏ *Sparkles glitter glue*

1. Marriage register

Pierce pattern 27 in carnation white card (8 x
9 cm). Stick this on blossom card and cut it out
so that there is a small border. Stick a strip of
wine red card (3 x 14.8 cm) on a strip of carnation
white card (3.5 x 14.8 cm) and stick this on a
violet double card. Stick the pattern on the right-
hand side of the card, the marriage register on
the left-hand side of the card and the cut out
hearts above the couple.

2. Congratulations

Pierce pattern 24 (page 22) in the back of the cut
out picture. Stick this on blossom card (8 x 8 cm)
and then on carnation white card (10.5 x 10.5 cm)

on which pattern 25 (page 23) has been pierced
in all the corners. Stick everything on a square
wine red double card.

3. Rectangles

Cut one rectangle (4.5 x 7 cm) out of blossom
card and one out of wine red card. Place them
on the inside of the front of the card in the top
left-hand and bottom right-hand corners. Draw
round them using a pencil. Pierce pattern 25
(page 23) four times in the empty spaces

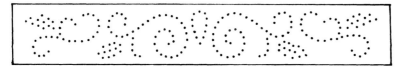

pattern 26

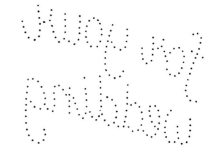

pattern 24

(see the photograph). Stick the pictures on the rectangles and stick these on the card.

4. Champagne bottle

Pierce pattern 27 (page 20) on carnation white card (8.5 x 13 cm). Cut a triangle out of the top right-hand corner (short sides 5 cm) and another triangle out of the bottom left-hand corner (short sides 5.5 cm). Stick this on wine red card (13.5 x 13.5 cm) and then on a blossom double card. Stick the cut out pictures in the corners.

5. Birds

Pierce pattern 5 (page 7) in carnation white card and cut it out. Stick this on violet card (9 x 9 cm) and then on wine red card (9.5 x 9.5 cm). Place the wine red card in the middle of the inside of the front of a carnation white double card (13 x 13 cm) and draw round it using a pencil. Mark the middle of the sides. Pierce pattern 26 (not the two outer branches) in the middle of every side. Stick the cut out pictures and the pattern on the card.

6. Bridal sweets

Pierce pattern 26 twice in carnation white card and cut out the patterns. Stick them on strips of wine red card (2.2 x 10.5 cm) and then on strips of blossom card (2.5 x 10.5 cm). Stick these strips on both sides of a violet double card. Stick the cut out picture on wine red card (4.5 x 4.5 cm). Stick this on blossom card (7 x 7 cm) and then stick this in the middle of the card.

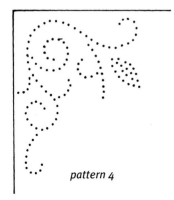

pattern 4

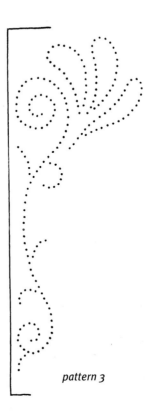

pattern 3

pattern 23

pattern 25

Butterflies

pattern 32

What you need:

- ❏ *Card: carnation white (no. 03), dark blue (no. 06) and daffodil (no. 28) (Papicolor) and green (Canson Mi-Teintes)*
- ❏ *Ornare cutting sheets (OK031, OK032 and OK034)*
- ❏ *Sparkles glitter glue*

1. Butterfly in a square

Pierce the body of pattern 32 in carnation white card and cut out the butterfly. Pierce the wings separately in carnation white card.
Cut them out and stick them on the cut out butterfly, using double-sided adhesive tape to stick them on the body and foam tape for the outside of the wings. Stick the cut out frame on blue card (5.8 x 5.8 cm) and stick this on green card (8 x 12.5 cm).
Stick this on carnation white card (8.5 x 13 cm) and stick everything on a yellow double card. Stick the cut out picture and the butterfly on the card.

2. Forget-me-nots

Pierce pattern 28 (page 27) in carnation white card and cut it out. Stick this on blue card (9 x 13.5 cm) and then on a green double card. Stick the cut out picture in the middle.

3. Tulips

Pierce pattern 31 (page 27) in carnation white card and cut it out. Stick this on green card (10 cm wide and 8 cm high on one side and 11 cm high on the other) and then on a blue double card. Stick the two cut out butterflies on the card.

4. White and yellow butterfly

Pierce the body of pattern 29 (page 26) in carnation white card and cut out the butterfly. Next, pierce only the outline of the wings in another carnation white card and cut out the wings separately. Pierce the inner parts of the wings in

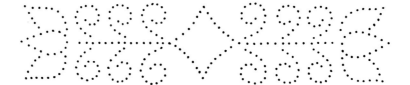

pattern 33

yellow card. Cut them out and stick them on both wings. Stick the wings on the body, using double-sided adhesive tape to stick them on the body and foam tape for the outside of the wings. Stick the cut out picture on blue card (7 x 7 cm). Stick this at an angle on yellow card (9 x 9 cm) and then on blue card (9.5 x 9.5 cm). Stick everything on a square green double card.

5. Cornflower

Pierce pattern 30 in carnation white card and cut it out. Pierce the top wing again in carnation white card and stick this on the butterfly, using double-sided adhesive tape to stick it to the body and foam tape at the top of the wing. Stick the cut out picture on green card (5 x 9 cm) and then on yellow card (5.5 x 9.5 cm). Stick this on the left-hand side of a blue double card. Draw a line

around the card using a white fine-liner and stick the butterfly on the card.

6. Two butterflies

Pierce two butterflies in carnation white card as described for card 1. Stick blue card (9 x 13 cm) on yellow card (9.5 x 13.5 cm) and stick this on a green double card. Stick the two butterflies, the flower and the four corner designs on the card.

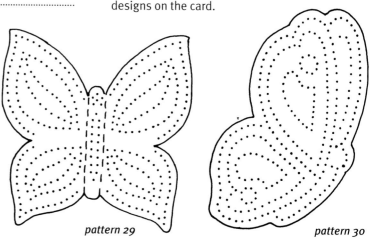

pattern 29
pattern 30

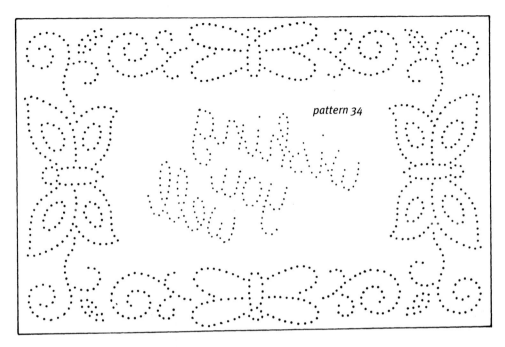

pattern 34

pattern 31

Fruit

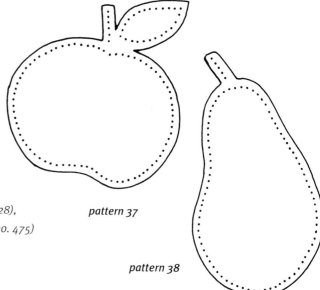

pattern 37

pattern 38

What you need:

❏ Card: carnation white (no. 03), daffodil (no. 28),
   olive green (no. 43) (Papicolor) and green (no. 475)
   (Canson Mi-Teintes)
❏ Ornare cutting sheets (OK011 and OK026)
❏ Sparkles glitter glue

pattern 35

1. Apples and pears

Pierce pattern 37 in green card and cut it out.
Pierce pattern 38 once in yellow card and once
in olive green card and cut them out. Stick the
cut out pictures in opposite corners of carnation
white card (8.5 x 13 cm) and stick the apple and
the pears in between. Stick the carnation white
card on yellow card (9 x 13.5 cm) and then stick
this on an olive green double card.

2. Petals

Pierce the line of petals of pattern 36 (page 30) in
yellow card. Cut it out and stick it on olive green
card (9 x 11 cm). Stick this on green card

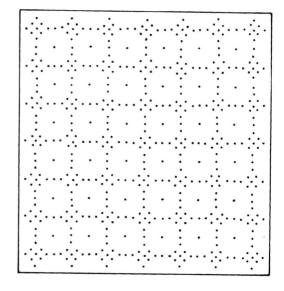

(10.5 x 11 cm) and then stick this on a carnation white double card. Stick the cut out picture in the middle.

3. A line of fruit

Pierce pattern 16 (page 11) in carnation white card and cut it out. Stick this on olive green card (7.5 x 12.5 cm) and then on a green double card. Stick the picture on yellow card (2.5 x 9 cm) and stick this in the middle of the card.

4. Best wishes

Pierce pattern 33 (page 26) in carnation white card (2.5 x 10.5 cm) and stick it on olive green card (3 x 11). Stick this on green card (3.5 x 11.5 cm) and then on the right-hand side of a yellow double card. Pierce pattern 34 (page 27) in the back of the picture and stick it on the card.

5. Square card

Pierce pattern 35 (page 28) in carnation white card (do not pierce the holes in the middle of the squares) and cut it out. Place it at an angle in the middle of a green card (12.5 x 12.5 cm) and draw around it using a pencil. Cut this shape out so that it is a couple of millimetres bigger. Stick olive green card (12 x 12 cm) behind the opening and stick the cut out pattern on this card. Stick four yellow triangles

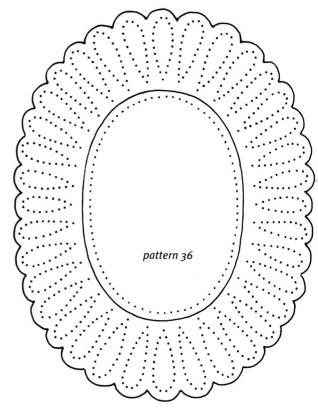

pattern 36

(short sides 4 cm) in the corners of the card and stick the cut out pictures on these squares.

6. Square pattern

Pierce pattern 35 (page 28) in carnation white card and cut it out. Stick this at the top of an olive green card (7.5 x 9.5 cm) and stick the picture at the bottom of the pattern, leaving a border of olive green on both sides. Stick this on green card (8 x 12 cm) and then on a yellow double card.

Christmas in 3D

What you need:

❏ *Card: carnation white (no. 03),*
   Christmas green (no. 18),
   caramel (no. 26) and nut brown (no. 39)
   (Papicolor)

❏ *3D cutting sheets*
   (3DA 3309 and 3DA 3310)

❏ *Sparkles glitter glue*

1. Basket on a landscape card

Pierce the corners of pattern 40 (page 34) in the four corners of carnation white card (8.5 x 12.5 cm). Stick this on green card (9 x 13 cm) and then on a brown double card. Stick the cut out picture in the middle.

2. Square card

Pierce pattern 40 (page 34) in carnation white card and cut it out. Stick this on green card (10 x 10 cm) and then on a caramel double card. Stick the cut out picture in the middle.

3. Lantern

Pierce pattern 39 (page 32) in carnation white card. Stick this on green card and cut it out so that there is a small border. Stick a strip of caramel card (6.3 x 12.5 cm) on the right-hand side of a square brown double card (13 x 13 cm). Stick the triangle in the middle of the card.

4. Yew tree

Pierce a border of pattern 40 (page 34) once at the top and once at the bottom of carnation white card (9 x 13.5 cm). Stick this on cream card (9.5 x 14 cm) and then on a green double card. Stick the cut out pictures in the middle of the card.

5. Basket on a portrait card

Draw a pencil line lengthways through the middle of the inside of a carnation white double card. Place brown card (5.5 x 5.5 cm) diagonally on this line (still on the back) 2.4 cm from the

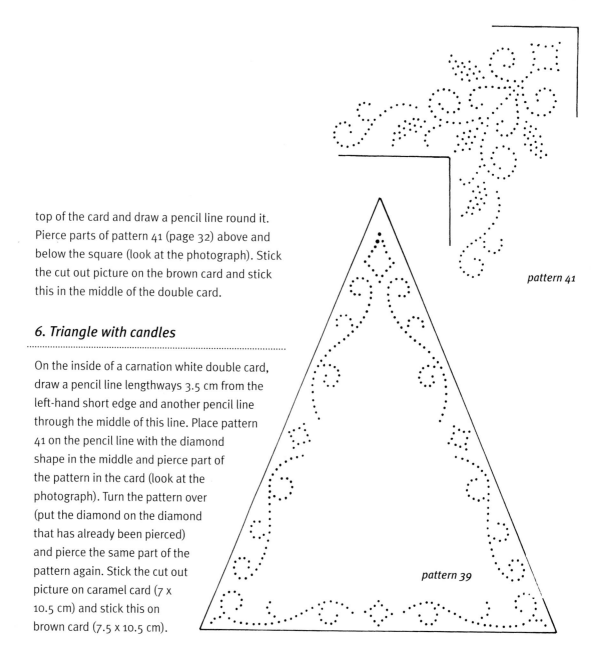

top of the card and draw a pencil line round it. Pierce parts of pattern 41 (page 32) above and below the square (look at the photograph). Stick the cut out picture on the brown card and stick this in the middle of the double card.

6. Triangle with candles

On the inside of a carnation white double card, draw a pencil line lengthways 3.5 cm from the left-hand short edge and another pencil line through the middle of this line. Place pattern 41 on the pencil line with the diamond shape in the middle and pierce part of the pattern in the card (look at the photograph). Turn the pattern over (put the diamond on the diamond that has already been pierced) and pierce the same part of the pattern again. Stick the cut out picture on caramel card (7 x 10.5 cm) and stick this on brown card (7.5 x 10.5 cm).

pattern 41

pattern 39

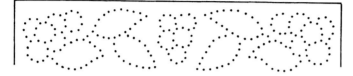

edge of pattern 40

pattern 40

pattern 43

Lilies

What you need:

❏ Card: carnation white (no. 03), heather (no. 22), pale pink (no. 23) and cerise (no. 33) (Papicolor)
❏ Ornare cutting sheets (OK021 and OK034)
❏ Sparkles glitter glue

An Ornare fan told us that the pierced holes are easy to feel and can, therefore, be read by the blind as Braille. He was kind enough to send us a couple of texts in Braille and we have used them in the following cards.
This is the meaning of the patterns which, of course, are printed as a mirror image.

44: Get well soon
45: Congratulations
46: Good luck
47: Consolation

1. Portrait card

Pierce pattern 48 (page 38) along the left-hand edge of a heather card. Pierce pattern 46 (page 38) in a pale pink card (5.5 x 10 cm). Stick this on a cerise card (6 x 10.5 cm) and then on a carnation white card (7.5 x 14.8 cm). Stick the cut out pictures on and then stick everything on the double card.

2. Squares

Pierce pattern 42 (page 36) twice in carnation white card (5 x 5 cm). Stick this, together with a pink and a heather square (5 x 5 cm), on a cerise card (11 x 11 cm). Stick everything on a pale pink double card. Stick the cut out pictures on the card.

3. Congratulations

Draw a pencil line inside a carnation white double card, 3.8 cm from the bottom of the card. Mark the middle of the line using the pencil and pierce pattern 41 (page 32) twice so that the diamond is at the intersection of the pencil lines. Pierce pattern 43 (page 35) in the cut out picture and stick it on cerise card (5 x 8 cm, so that

you can see the holes better). Stick this on
the double card.

4. Landscape card

Pierce pattern 45 (page 38) in pale pink card
(4 x 10 cm) which has had a line of holes pierced
around the edge. Stick this at an angle on a
cerise card (7 x 11.5 cm) and then on a carnation
white card (7.5 x 12 cm). Pierce pattern 25
(page 23) in every corner of a heather double
card. Stick everything, including the cut out
picture, on the card.

5. Square with diagonal lines

Pierce pattern 42 in the top left-hand and bottom
right-hand corners of a square pale pink double
card. Cut a strip out of carnation white card (3.5 x
19 cm) and stick it on a strip of cerise card (4 x
19 cm). Stick this diagonally on the card and cut off
any excess. Stick the cut out picture on the card.

pattern 42

6. Flower

Pierce part of the petal border of pattern 36
(page 30) (every other petal) in carnation white
card (9 x 11.5 cm). Stick this on heather card
(9.5 x 12 cm) and then on a cerise double card.
Pierce the oval of pattern 36 (page 30) in a
heather card. Cut it out and stick it on the card
together with the cut out pictures.

pattern 48

Stick the braille texts on the back of the card and pierce them well.
At the front of the card they will be "readable" then.

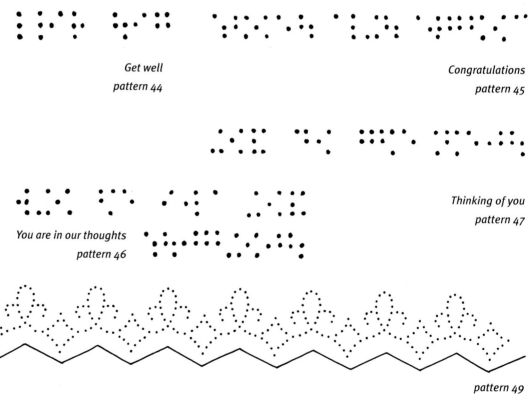

Get well
pattern 44

Congratulations
pattern 45

Thinking of you
pattern 47

You are in our thoughts
pattern 46

pattern 49

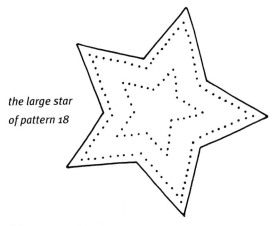

*the large star
of pattern 18*

Landscapes

What you need:

- ❏ Card: snowy white (no. 30),
  night blue (no. 41) and ice blue (42)
  (Papicolor)
- ❏ Ornare cutting sheet OK030,
- ❏ Sparkles glitter glue

1. Christmas tree and star

Pierce pattern 19 (page 15) and the large
star of pattern 18 in snowy white card and
cut them out. Stick the picture on night
blue card (5 x 1 cm) and stick this on an
ice blue double card.
Stick the patterns on the card.

2. Square card with a square pattern

Pierce pattern 35 (page 28) in snowy white
card and cut it out. Stick this at an angle on
night blue card (10 x 10 cm) and then on an
ice blue double card. Stick the cut out pictures
in the corners.

3. Portrait card with a frame

Pierce pattern 13 (page 11) in snowy white card
and cut it out. Stick this on ice blue card (9 x
12 cm) and then on a night blue double card.

4. Square card with a diagonal pattern

Pierce pattern 41 (page 32) twice in opposite
corners of snowy white card (11 x 11 cm). Stick the
cut out picture on night blue card (3.8 x 3.8 cm) in
the middle of the snowy white card and stick everything on night blue card (11.5 x 11.5 cm). Finally,
stick everything on a square ice blue double card.

5. Ice blue portrait card

Pierce pattern 3 (page 23) twice in an ice blue
double card. Stick the picture on night blue
card (3.5 x 8 cm) and stick this on snowy white
card (4 x 8.5 cm). Finally, stick everything on the
double card.

6. Landscape card

Pierce pattern 49 in snowy white card (7 x
14.8 cm) and cut it out. Stick this and the cut
out picture on a night blue double card.

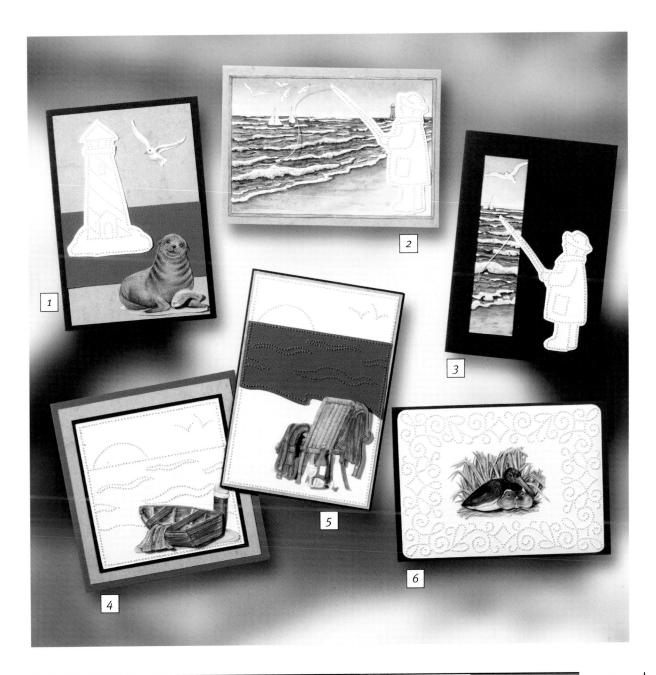

The sea

What you need:
- ❏ *Card: carnation white (no. 03), dark blue (no. 06) and night blue (no. 41) (Papicolor) and parchment*
- ❏ *3D cutting sheet (3D394)*
- ❏ *3D background sheet (3DA3308)*

1. Lighthouse

Stick dark blue card (5 x 9.5 cm) 2.5 cm from the bottom of parchment card (9.5 x 14 cm). Stick this on a night blue double card. Pierce pattern 50 in carnation white card. Cut it out and stick it, together with the cut out pictures, on the card.

2. Fisherman on a landscape card

Pierce pattern 52 in carnation white card and cut it out. Stick white cord on the back of the rod. Thread the cord through the last hole in the rod from the back to the front. Stick the fisherman on the 3D background and thread the cord (using a needle) through the 3D back-ground and stick it to the back using a piece of adhesive tape. Stick the background on a parchment double card.

3. Fisherman on a portrait card

Pierce pattern 52 in carnation white card and cut it out. Cut a rectangle (3 x 11.7 cm) out of a night blue double card 1.5 cm from the top, bottom and left-hand side. Cut a 3D background lengthways through the middle and stick a part of it behind the opening. Stick the fisherman on the card and fix a white cord to the rod (see card 2).

4. Sunset on a square card

Pierce pattern 51 (page 48) in carnation white card and cut it out. Stick this on night blue card (10.5 x 10.5 cm) and then on parchment card (12 x 12 cm). Finally, stick this on a dark blue double card. Stick the cut out picture on the card.

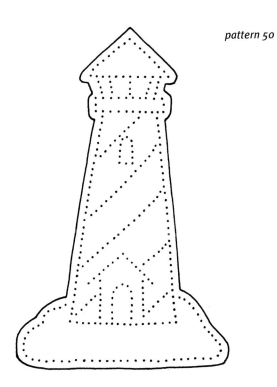

pattern 50

pattern 52

5. Sunset on a portrait card

Pierce the sea section of pattern 51 (page 48) in dark blue card and cut it out. Pierce the top part of the pattern on the top of carnation white card (10 x 14.3 cm) and the bottom part on the bottom of the carnation white card. Stick the sea section on top of this and cut the edges off, remaining as close as possible to the pierced outer lines.
Stick this on parchment card (10 x 14.3 cm) and then on a night blue double card. Stick the cut out picture on the card.

6. Sea bird with young

Pierce pattern 55 (page 46) in carnation white card and cut it out. Do not cut out the inner rectangle and round off the corners.
Stick the cut out picture on the pattern and then stick this on a night blue double card.

In the garden

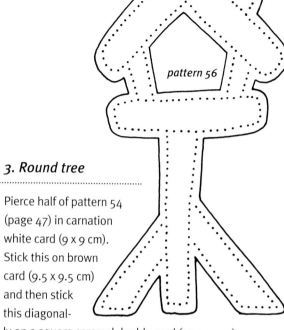

pattern 56

What you need:
- ❏ Card: carnation white (no. 03),
  Christmas green (no. 18),
  caramel (no. 26) and nut brown (no. 39)
  (Papicolor)
- ❏ 3D cutting sheets (3D388 and 3D392)

1. Birdhouse

Pierce pattern 56 in carnation white card and cut it out. Stick this and the cut out pictures on brown card (9 x 13.5 cm) and then on green card (9.5 x 14 cm). Finally, stick this on a caramel double card.

2. Garden chair

Pierce pattern 53 (page 47) in carnation white card (12.5 x 12.5 cm) and stick this on a square brown double card (13 x 13 cm). Stick the cut out picture in the middle of green card (8 x 8 cm) and then on caramel card (8.5 x 8.5 cm).

3. Round tree

Pierce half of pattern 54 (page 47) in carnation white card (9 x 9 cm). Stick this on brown card (9.5 x 9.5 cm) and then stick this diagonally on a square caramel double card (14 x 14 cm). Stick the cut out picture on the card.

4. Fountain

Pierce pattern 55 (page 46) in carnation white card and cut it out. Stick this on a green double card and stick the cut out picture in the middle.

5. Toolbox

Stick a strip of caramel card and a strip of green card (both 3.5 x 14.5 cm) on a brown double card. Pierce pattern 54 (page 47) in carnation

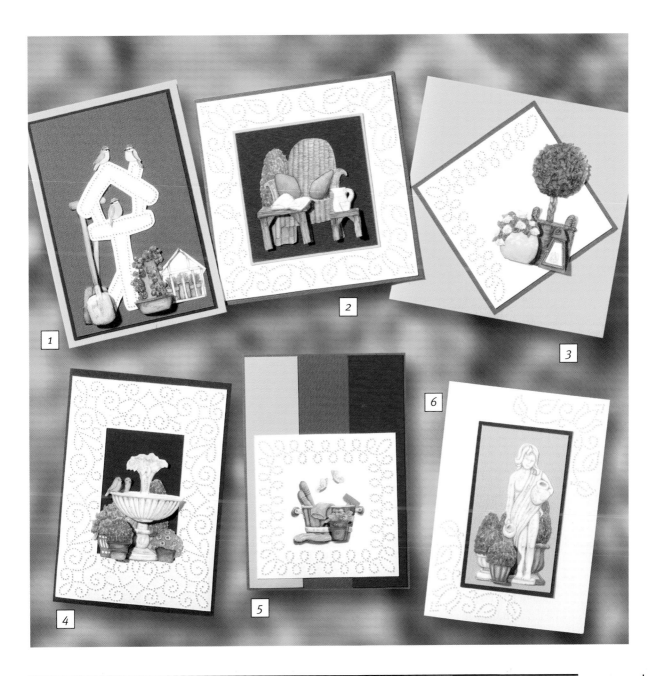

white card (9 x 9 cm). Stick this on the card and stick the cut out picture in the middle.

6. Sculpture

Pierce a corner of pattern 53 in the top right-hand and bottom left-hand corners of a carnation white

double card. Stick the cut out picture on caramel card (5.5 x 10 cm) and then on green card (6 x 10.5 cm). Finally, stick this in the middle of the double card.

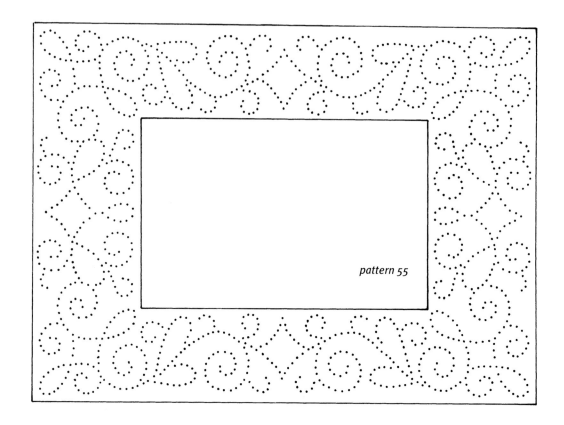

pattern 55

outer border pattern 53
inner border pattern 54

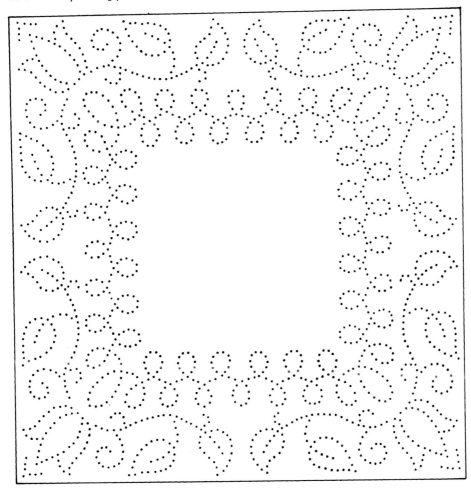

continuation of page 7

5. Circle of flowers

Pierce pattern 4 (page 23) in all four corners of a carnation white card (10 x 10 cm). Stick this on violet card (10.5 x 10.5 cm) and then on a cerise double card. Stick the picture in the middle.

6. Oval of flowers

Pierce pattern 1 (page 6) in carnation white card and cut it out. Stick this on cerise card (9 x 13 cm) and then on caramel card (9.5 x 13.4 cm). Finally, stick this on a violet double card.

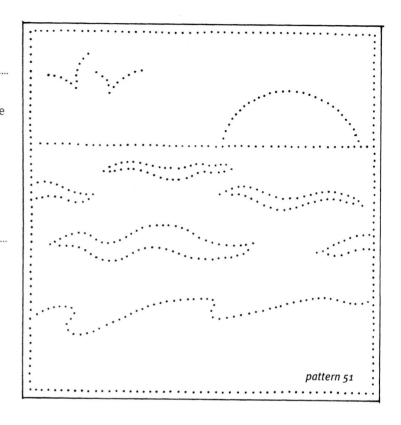

pattern 51

continuation of page 12
pencil to draw the outline of this opening on the white card. Pierce pattern 16 (page 11) in the carnation white card and stick this behind the opening in the red card. Stick the cut out picture on blue card (2.8 x 9.4 cm) and stick this in the middle of the card.

6. Champagne bottle

Pierce pattern 13 (page 11) in carnation white card and cut it out. Stick this on blue card (8.5 x 11.5 cm) and then on red card (9.2 x 12.2 cm). Finally, stick this on a square green double card.